BUSTA RHYME

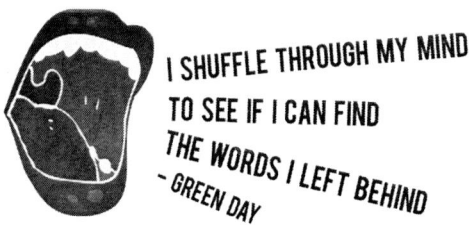

I SHUFFLE THROUGH MY MIND
TO SEE IF I CAN FIND
THE WORDS I LEFT BEHIND
~ GREEN DAY

WALES

Edited By Sheila Ashwood

First published in Great Britain in 2017 by:

 Young**Writers** Est. 1991

Coltsfoot Drive
Peterborough
PE2 9BF
Telephone: 01733 890066
Website: www.youngwriters.co.uk

FOREWORD

Welcome Reader,

For Young Writers' latest competition, *Busta Rhyme*, we challenged secondary school pupils to take inspiration from the world around them, whether from the news, their own lives or even songs, and write a poem on any subject of their choice. They rose to the challenge magnificently, with young writers up and down the country displaying their poetic flair.

We chose poems for publication based on style, expression, imagination and technical skill. The result is this entertaining collection full of diverse and imaginative poetry which covers a variety of topics - from favourite things and seasons to more serious subjects such as bullying and war. Using poetry as their tool, the young writers have taken this opportunity to express their thoughts and feelings through verse. This anthology is also a delightful keepsake to look back on in years to come.

Here at Young Writers our aim is to encourage creativity in the next generation and to inspire a love of the written word, so it's great to get such an amazing response, with some absolutely fantastic poems. I'd like to congratulate all the young poets in *Busta Rhyme - Wales* - I hope this inspires them to continue with their creative writing.

Sheila Ashwood

CONTENTS

Lewis Vaughan (13)	82
Thomas Jonathan Davies (14)	84
Emily Cann (14)	85
Cory Ford (13)	86
Harriet Beattie (13)	87
Joshua Smith (14)	88
Thomas Lamb (13)	89
Alfie Sewell (13)	90
Lauren May Thompson (13)	91
Anna Rose Borley (13)	92
George John (13)	93
Tom Bridge (13)	94
Callum Porteous (13)	95
Kim Emily Brown (13)	96
Anna Jenkins Delf (13)	97

Pencoed Comprehensive School, Bridgend

Jade Evans	98
Thomas Lloyd Freeman-Jones (12)	99
Nakita Mayle	100
Molly Harris	101
Bradley David John Withers (12)	102
Kira Paul	103
Morgan Poole (13)	104
Jack Morris	105
Roan Burnett	106
Ellis Jones (12)	107
Georgina Austin	108
Taine Josif Evans (12)	109
Ioan Whittington (12)	110
Llŷr Aeron Harries (12)	111

St Illtyd's Catholic High School, Cardiff

| Holly Tee (12) | 112 |

Ysgol Aberconwy, Conwy

| Kaitlyn Davies (13) | 115 |
| Ruth Dean (15) | 116 |

Aiden James Jones (15)	119
Ffion Harrison-Boothby (15)	120
Aron Jones (11)	122
James Todd (12)	124
Malin Owen (12)	127
Ruby Rose Rinaldi (11)	128
Charlotte Stevenson (15)	130
David Lewis (14)	132
Ben Ahari (12)	134
Amy Davis (12)	136
Ashleigh Hughes (12)	138
Daniel Roberts (14)	140
Violet Holly Paton (11)	142
Tegan Haf Simpson (14)	143
Lydia Smith (12)	144
Alice Dyson (14)	145
Emma Buckley (15)	146
Sam Roberts (14)	148
Cian Whitlow (15)	149
April Ehlke-West (14)	150
Jake Ethan Bing (12)	151
Benn Lundstram (14)	152
Mary Jones (14)	153
Charlotte Lewis (15)	154
Sioned Jones (14)	155
Daniel Godawa (12)	156
Erin Hughes (12)	157
Matilda Cockrill (11)	158
Thomas Taylor (11)	159
Stephanie Leigh Stocks (11)	160
Callum Roberts (11)	161
Sophie Maloney (11)	162
Rachel Lauren Roberts (14)	163
Macy Hughes (11)	164
Hannah J (11)	165
Lana Jessica Davidson-Flood (15)	166

THE POEMS

In life it's good to be curious, always seeking new,
Asking questions, getting answers and travelling too.
All these things enrich your life,
Expand your knowledge, ideas rife.
Life is precious, life can be kind
You need curiosity to open your mind.

Tia Hughes (13)

Cwmbran High School, Cwmbran

I Am Black

Tall Old Sam, such a fool,
Always bullied Matise at school.
Matise was dark and never went out.
He always came home to hear his father shout.

Sam was light and would always brag.
He always had the new hype bag!

Sam hit and hurt Matise.
All he wanted was a bit of peace!
He shouted out, 'Black' and
Threatened to stab him in the back!

Matise wouldn't tell any of his teachers
Thinking that Sam would make new preachers.

They called him 'Monkey Boy' and threw out rope.
Wondering how he would ever cope!
He shouted out, 'Black'
Saying that they would burn down his poor little shack!

Matise stood up on his window pane,
Thinking that he was going insane.
This is the message that he wanted to send,
As he knew his life was coming to an end.

I am African
I am proud
I have rights
I am black.

These were the words that he once sung,
As he fell as he fell and solemnly hung.

Dylan Taylor (12)
Cwmbran High School, Cwmbran

Change

Hey,
It's been a while
I still refuse to change,
Living with my awesome ways
You still don't believe in fairy tales,
Or ghouls and ghosts.
But I still live in my childish dreams,
Stuck in a fantasy.

Hey,
What happened to everything,
The cartwheels and the tricks
The faces that we pulled at passing cars
And often playing air guitar.
We had a blast on the street
Mischievous and cunning we would be.

Hey, please don't go away,
It's no fun,
I'm a little bit stunned
You no longer want to be young.
Grown-ups are so boring,
All they do is count.

Let's stay young forever,
I still refuse to change.
Let's never be grown ups
It's possible
Peter Pan did it, so we can too
Let's stay young forever,
We still refuse to change.

Summer Bowen Quirk

Cwmbran High School, Cwmbran

One Day

'How many more?' she says
As the bullets rain down
'I don't know,' he replies
With a melancholic frown.

A massacre of race,
As the gunmen parade through the city
No help or guidance
Will anyone have pity?

She begins to cry
With her hands on her face
Her school, house, family are destroyed
The world is a disgrace.

Then suddenly the ambush stops
Dad looks at the damage they have made
He can only hear screams.
He is angry, not afraid.

The dust attacks his senses
Like he is buried in sand
So many innocent lives stolen
How can beliefs ruin a land?

Dad walks to comfort his daughter
With her head resting on her knee.
He wraps his arms around her and promises,
'One day we will be free.'

Rhys Nicholson (13)
Cwmbran High School, Cwmbran

Dogs

Some dogs are big, some dogs are small,
No matter what, I love them all.
Some dogs are fluffy, some dogs are smooth
And really do have great moves.

No matter if you like them,
Or maybe do not,
They will always be cute,
And you maybe not.

Some can be clean, some can be messy,
Most are kind, some are aggressive.

Some are tall as, some are small and all could
laugh all day,
Some roll over and like to have fun,
Some like to lunch and play in the sun.

No matter if you like them or maybe
Do not.
They will always be cute and you
maybe not!

Even if you don't like dogs
Give them love and you'll see what...

Some dogs are big, some dogs are small
But no matter what I love them all...

Emily Farrington
Cwmbran High School, Cwmbran

Words Can Hurt

This is a poem about Lilly
Lilly is a normal, kind girl,
Being bullied, they make her sad, depressed, hurt
She thinks, *what have I done to them?*

She's alone, sat in a corner, drowning herself in tears,
Lilly's afraid to tell anyone, people laugh at her,
Teachers don't even notice her,
She gets called ugly, geek, stupid,
She thinks, *what have I done to them?*

She wants to stick up for herself,
She just can't, Lilly says to herself,
What have I done to them?
They hit her with more hurtful, careless words,
Loner, cry baby.

She is starting to build her confidence up,
She actually went to the teacher and told them
What's been going on,
Remember, be a buddy not a bully.

Emma Bridgeman (11)
Cwmbran High School, Cwmbran

Miss You

We've known each other for so long,
But now you're leaving, I must stay strong,
I'm not sure how I'll manage, I guess I'll have to cope,
I hope you come back, I hope and hope.

Your voice is jammed into my head,
The kind and inspirational words you said,
Your laugh and your smile is the one thing I miss,
I miss everything about you, I miss, I miss.

I hope you're loving life in your new home,
But don't forget all the friends you had to let go,
I'm thinking about you every second, every day,
Come back and visit, I wish you could have stayed.

The time has come to let you go,
So I just wanted to let you know,
All of the amazing memories we have made,
I hope and I know they'll never fade.

Maia Elsworthy (11)
Cwmbran High School, Cwmbran

Friends Are Like Leaves

Leaves? Never thought of your best friend like a leaf!
Well friends have fights, but most always come back!
Like trees they lose leaves and mostly always get them back
(Unless the tree is dying).
Death is like the bully for the tree, no one wants to die, do they?
As for us, nobody wants to get bullied, it isn't fun for anyone!
So why do they do it?
Because they're not strong, they see your weakness,
And just try to bring you down!
They also may do it for fun,
Or just because they are being bullied too.

So why do we cut down trees?

We cut them down for practically the same reasons,
Self-enjoyment, for paper and homes.

We're the bully to the trees,
We're getting rid of what was given to us years ago!

Jessica Susan Baker (11)
Cwmbran High School, Cwmbran

You Be You

What has the world come to?
All this wrong that people do,
Just for the image they want to show
Down the evil path they go
People come in all shapes and sizes,
Being a bully doesn't come with prizes.
Your identity should be your own,
As a better person you will be known
Words can hurt, makes me sad,
When I have done nothing bad.

Words can hurt, don't know why,
All I know is that they make me cry.
The next person they go hurt,
Or try to make them feel like dirt.
The words they say do upset me,
Why don't you just let me be?
Find the courage, speak up and tell,
Then maybe things will turn out well.
Remember next time you be you,
Your friends will be there to help you through!

Ruby Gibbins (12)
Cwmbran High School, Cwmbran

Untitled

I just want to skate but you might not rate
Even now my skills are considered as great
I'm going down the skatepark and staying till late
Until I land this kickflip on the griptape
Going to keep trying, even if I fail
Straight back to my feet, then up onto the rail
Skating every day, I'm not afraid to bail
It's Louis on the mic coming straight out of Wales
It's Louis on the mic, you better get ready
I'm the best MC 'cause you know I keep it steady
Every day I play Xbox on the telly
And I have a bath every night so I'm not smelly
Listen up people I'm the king of rapping
And everybody in school calls me the captain
Got a captain's badge on my chest
And everybody knows red house is the best.

Louis Bourne (11)
Cwmbran High School, Cwmbran

Racism

You're black, I'm white
We are all the same,
Problems between us are a terrible shame,
We are all God's angels,
No matter our colour,
He looks out for us,
And wants us to be brothers,
Chinese, Asian, French,
What's the problem?

We should treat each other the same,
No one's different,
Our colours don't matter,
Religions neither.

The whole world is at breaking point,
The violence, the hurt, try as we might,
We can't seem to put an end to the pain,
The governments and presidents try in vain.

We need to pull all together
To put an end to all the terror,
Let the whole world smile together,
And live in peace and harmony, forever.

Alice Virgo (11)
Cwmbran High School, Cwmbran

Why?

Why is there such a thing as bullying?
There's no point in doing it, it's not a good thing.
Yeah, some are different but we all feel the same way inside.
Some are small, some are tall,
Some are loud, some are shy!
Different people are different sizes and weight
So if you're a bully just be kind and be their mate.
We all should be against the bullies out there
Only if everyone cared
I bet it's horrible to get bullied and to be sad every day.
I hope if you see someone getting bullied
You would help anyway.
I'm sorry if you're being bullied out there
Please just stick up for yourself, don't be scared.
So now think before you do
And then the world will be a better place for me and you.

Maci Mayo (12)
Cwmbran High School, Cwmbran

Jack

Bang, bang, bang!
Three knocks at the door,
A whisper of silence,
Through the hall,
Expecting certain violence,
Fear sets in, no one to cull.

Footsteps getting louder, afraid to turn my back,
Moving from room to room anxiously
Not wanting to be the next victim
Of the Ripper, known as Jack...

A deadly screech filled my ears with pain
Jack was at it again
The creak of the oak wood stairs
Lifting the tips of my hair
Panicking, I searched for somewhere to hide
Unable to cope, I lost all my pride.

I escaped that night
It sure did give me a fright
Just watch your back
Because he's on the loose
Look out for Jack!

Ellie Louise Harris (11)
Cwmbran High School, Cwmbran

Football

Stepping onto the field getting ready to play we stand in
position.
When we are ready the referee blows the whistle and people
take the kick off.
Then people start to sprint towards the ball and people
tackle the ball,
Kick the ball to score.
I feel the wind blowing through my hair and I smile as I
score then I run off to celebrate and I hear the shouts from
the crowd.
And off we run to do it again
With that buzzing feeling from the last goal to push us on to
score again.
When the game is all over the feeling of satisfaction makes
me grin
And my mum frowns to see the dirty clothes.
We gather up to say well done to the other team
And celebrate together that we won.

Shane Groves (11)
Cwmbran High School, Cwmbran

My Dog Buddy

When you were a puppy you were so cute
But then you ate my shoes
My mum went mad, it made me sad
I really had the blues

You run and you jump
And bounce around
No better friend
Have I found

A smile on your face
A twinkle in your eye
You're so sweet
No need to ask why

You wag your tail so fast
Like a speeding propeller
You are my best friend
You really are my 'little fella'

We love to do things together
Especially getting muddy
You are my pal forever
That's why I named you *Buddy.*

Scott Kenneth McDonald (11)
Cwmbran High School, Cwmbran

My World

The sky glows a bright ombre dawn
Coated with angelic tears of rain,
Fading through the mountains
Houses, apartments, scattered randomly with an
unidentified form
In, inhabits people tall and small, wide or thin
They seem different when they start to complain.
When they don't realise they're exactly the same!
Whether you can't or can, it's not an option.
You have to figure out that we have different personalities.
Inside or outside comes from within
Beauty shines through when generosity and affection
passes on,
You may be different, but you're still you.

Melissa Lena Henderson (11)

Cwmbran High School, Cwmbran

Say No To Drugs

Sitting around taking drugs
Sniffing the food meant for mugs
Snorting it, smoking it, injecting it too,
The types of things a fool would do.

Heroin, crack, smack and coke
Injecting it up, smoking a tote
Pushing the poison into their vein
When they're without it they go insane.

Robbing the innocent to fund their next fix
Actions like this make me feel sick
A round of applause for those who get clean
The demons of drugs can be so mean
Don't be a fool, just say, 'No!'
Be stronger than peer pressure, give it a go.

Brody Jae Waite (11)
Cwmbran High School, Cwmbran

Bullying

Bullying, a word that is known with a lot of kids,
This word resembles fighting and name-calling.
Can't these bullies understand that fighting is not right?
It's just wrong,
Whenever you see someone getting bullied, don't react.
It will make things worse and then you'll get the blame,
So if you see your friend getting bullied or anyone.
Just tell someone.
Bullying.
A word that disgusts people, a word that describes
Fighting, name calling and even racism.
This is a word that infects you with harmful comments.

Thomas Daniel Lewis (11)
Cwmbran High School, Cwmbran

Bullying

It's happening all around,
Pushing kids onto the cold, hard ground.
Physical, verbal, social and cyber,
We should not have to possess this fear,
We should not have to cry those tears,
And not have to fight,
Shedding tears and blood-curdling cries,
Just try to see it from someone else's eyes,
We shouldn't have to feel this low,
And have bruises and scratches to show,
Stand up and let this message spread,
Hurry, before someone winds up dead.

Ellie Mathias (12)
Cwmbran High School, Cwmbran

Don't Be Sexist

There should be no difference
Between a boy and a girl
And this rule should apply
To the whole of the world.

Cooking, cleaning,
Sewing and knitting
Boys' things, girls' things
There should be no splitting.

Driving tractors or trucks
Being a nurse or a teacher
Are jobs for anyone
Regardless of gender.

Don't be sexist
It's not cool,
It's dumb
And really cruel.

Ethan Todd (11)
Cwmbran High School, Cwmbran

A Letter For Bampy

God looked across his Heavens,
And found an empty space
He gazed upon his earth,
Before he noticed your humble face.
He held his arms around you,
And soon lifted you to rest.
Are his Heavens truly beautiful?
I heard he only takes the best.

We thought of you today,
We insist that's nothing new.
We thought of you yesterday,
And the days before that too.
We think of you in silence,
We often speak your name.

Holly-Marie Greening (11)
Cwmbran High School, Cwmbran

Honesty

Honesty is something good
It helps us a lot with life
You should tell the naked truth
Instead of telling a fully dressed lie
Honesty is good
Lying is bad
If you tell the truth you'll get through life
But if you tell a lie then you'll be in trouble
Honesty, honesty, honesty,
Go on, give it a go
You'll be in more trouble for telling a lie
Than telling the truth
So do it right and tell the honesty in what you did.

Daniel Cowin (11)
Cwmbran High School, Cwmbran

Bullying Harris

Bullying is bad
Bullying's not fair
Do you see that girl standing over there?
Is she pretty or is she not?
Does it matter about her looks?

Bullying is bad
Bullying's not fair
Did you make that girl cry over there?
If you did then be ashamed
But if you didn't then you're okay.

Bullying is bad
Bullying isn't right
You shouldn't make anyone cry
That's just not right.

Isabel Harris (13)
Cwmbran High School, Cwmbran

Beauty

A beauty that comes from within,
Is a beauty that age cannot wrinkle.
Not distracted by a single pimple,
But a radiance of joy and judgement.
A person of inner beauty,
A person judged by beauty, by society.
Their sweet smile will never fade away.

They long for a pure heart,
And wear a cheerful look.
Even though her smile is big,
Her confidence is small,
For her beauty isn't judged within after all.

Elise Phillips (12)
Cwmbran High School, Cwmbran

Dobby

Dobby was the greatest elf to live,
And he gave all the help
That he could ever give

Dobby was a hero,
But when his heart rate came to zero,
He was soon to go.

Dobby had green eyes,
And he listened to his master's cries,
As he stared up at the sky,
Then it was time to die.

Dobby was the greatest elf to live
And gave all the help
That he could ever give.

Mya Arwen Francis (12)
Cwmbran High School, Cwmbran

Friendship

Friendship is about who you can trust and rely on
And who can put a smile on your face
When it's your worst day and when you're down
And someone who can have a laugh
And someone who you can have a gossip with
And share different stuff, have days out together and
sleepovers
Someone to talk to if anything is wrong
And you may have arguments
But will always make up and be as close as you are.

Caitlyn Davies (14)
Cwmbran High School, Cwmbran

Comp

At first it's big and it's loud,
Making you go round and round,
You make decisions good and bad,
You feel like you're going mad!

Comp is fun and is new.
Doing things all for you,
After all it is a ball,
Even if you're pushed to the wall.

You'll have some work,
But never be a total jerk,
Revise for your test,
And make sure you do your very best!

Lilly Adams (11)
Cwmbran High School, Cwmbran

Perfect

People may look and stare
But you know they'll never care.
From your head to your feet, heart to brain,
People are mostly all the same.
'Fat', 'ugly', 'stupid' and 'nerd,'
We all know they're just words!

Everyone is perfect in their little own way.
Bisexual, straight, pan or gay.
Boy, girl, both or neither,
Self hate is not good for any creature.

Neve Taylor Jenkins (12)
Cwmbran High School, Cwmbran

Best Friends

Until you came
Into my world
There was nothing but
Darkness and gloom.
My world is missing
The stars and moon.

The passion between us
Is strong
The secrets and inside jokes
Will keep going on.

That's me and my best friend's story
Trust me, there will be more
That's the beginning,
Many more things to be made
Me and my best friend.

Abbie-May Allford (11)
Cwmbran High School, Cwmbran

WWII Sorrows

I hear bombs in the night,
I hear screams that give me a fright

Bang! Bang! goes the gun,
I hope I don't hear another one.

As the door starts to creak,
I open the window to take a peek.

I open the door and walk around,
All of a sudden I hear a sound.

Then I found a man dead,
He was my close friend named Fred.

Aaron James (13)
Cwmbran High School, Cwmbran

Friends

We call one a friend, but are they?
One can be so mean,
And one can be so kind.
We have a best friend so true
But we also have a friend
Who turns on you some day.
We have enemies who used to be friends.
So sad, too sad and just because you have a new friend.
Make sure who you trust,
Make sure they are not horrible.
Find a friend who will stay friends forever.

Riley Fullick (11)
Cwmbran High School, Cwmbran

Colour

Black, white, any colour,
People have different skin colours,
People use it against each other
To hurt one another,
Even to declare war on each other.
Pain and suffering has been caused
Through the hate against each other
Death has grown on people because of racism,
People have been sent into war
People have lost family
Because of their skin colour.

Katie-Ann James (12)
Cwmbran High School, Cwmbran

Where Will The World Take Me?

To the top of the mountain,
Or the bottom of a hill,
Maybe I will be spending my days
Counting dollar bills
Or in a movie in Beverly Hills.

Where will the world take me?
Chasing my wildest dream or
Watching my children's sports teams
I don't care if I'm changing my child's nappy,
As long as I'm happy!

Amy Jones (11)
Cwmbran High School, Cwmbran

Change

We live with changes every day
No matter how big or small they will always creep round.

Change will affect us in a way which will change us
Many changes we can get used to but it's sometimes impossible.

Change is essential and is needed to make people happier
Some change can be changed, but comes with a consequence.

Tyler Morton (11)
Cwmbran High School, Cwmbran

Robots

Robots are cool, robots are grand,
Robots will always give a hand,
Some are big, some are small,
But that doesn't matter at all.
Some are brainy, some are thick,
Some are slow, some are quick,
Some are tiny, some are shiny,
Some are dark, some are sharp.
So robots are cool, robots are grand
Robots are a helping hand.

Lewis Williams (11)
Cwmbran High School, Cwmbran

Education

Education is important for our future
Even when you may need a tutor
So try and do well in all your exams
And you will have lots of exciting plans
Maths and English are your mains
That's probably why there are so many games
Live, laugh and learn and live your life as you choose
It's all mapped out, you'll never lose.

Charlotte Erasmus (11)
Cwmbran High School, Cwmbran

Weather

Weather will never bring you down
Only when it's hammering down
When the sun is up it's time to have some fun.
When the weather is OK, it's time to run away
When it is misty have a little picnic
When I'm very hot, don't forget your sun block.
It's time to say goodbye because the moon is saying hello.

Taylor Porter (13)
Cwmbran High School, Cwmbran

Environment

Bang, bang goes the gun
I bet they are having so much fun.

Destroying the city
Through and through

The wind blew and blew
Hey, I hope they don't find us too.

Run, run, I hear,
I hope they don't know we are near.

Bang, bang, I am gone.

Elle Challingsworth (13)
Cwmbran High School, Cwmbran

Stereotypes

If a boy wears pink he's gay
If someone listens to rock music they're a goth
If a girl wears pink she's a girly girl
If she's a girl she's bad at sports
If you're a girl you only care about your appearance
There is a stereotype for everything
Let people be who they want to be and don't judge.

Carys Groves (13)
Cwmbran High School, Cwmbran

Life

Life, earth, land, ocean,
Universe, galaxy,
All features of life.
How did it start?
When will it end?
What big events have happened?
And what's going to happen?
But most importantly, what's happening now?
Is Earth different?
Is Earth unique?
What is Earth?
All questions of life.

Abigail Elizabeth Brown (12)
Cwmbran High School, Cwmbran

Size

Does size matter?
Why can't you just be wise
Does size affect the person's personality? No!
Be nice, whether fat, skinny, thick or thin,
Size is just a person's frame.
They can still be kind
Bullies are like bulls
They are fierce and irritating,
Leave them alone!

Rebekah Proctor (14)
Cwmbran High School, Cwmbran

Friendship

Always have a friend,
Never, never turn the bend on them.

Always be a friend,
Never know when you get the best of friends.

Always be the better friend,
Because they will try to be better.

Never be mean,
Or you might just fall out.

Bobby John Stallard (11)

Cwmbran High School, Cwmbran

Football

Life is a game, football is serious.
If at first you don't succeed, it's because of me.
A day without football is a day wasted.
I'll let my feet do the talking.
It's the most popular sport for a reason.
Not just a sport, an obsession.

Max Tucker
Cwmbran High School, Cwmbran

Barcelona

Over eleven players playing in each match,
You've got Messi, Squires, Neymer and a lot more.
First in the league, can't get beat, can't get knocked out.
Best division in the Spanish League
Better than Real Madrid, better than the rest.

Jake Williams
Cwmbran High School, Cwmbran

Reign Of Fire

For every dragon that lights the farmland
To every human that keeps his ground
And every animal will perish
As time will only turn around yeah,
When we dented our lives
As I think we will win
Every dragon will die.

Riley Francis (11)
Cwmbran High School, Cwmbran

Untitled

It's always a struggle to get out of bed
As you cry out, 'Mum, please, let me rest my head.'
We dress in our houses in black, white and purple
And smart trousers and blazers,
Pity summer is over so soon.

Gary Phillips (13)
Cwmbran High School, Cwmbran

Pain

In a nest, lays a bird,
Newly born, it lets out a chirp.
Its little wings, all frail and white,
One day it'll grow and learn to fly.

Though the peace of the wood is soon disturbed,
As along comes the machinery, with its fiery burn.
The trees and leaves, tumble to the ground,
Mother Nature's kingdom is falling down.

As the humans come to take their land,
The animals panic, and run around.
Mother bird flees, flying high in the sky,
But she's leaving her baby, leaving it to die.

Though zoos may seem like a great place to be
The animals cry, trapped, in captivity.
As the people stare and their cameras click,
The animals think of the life they could live.

As they lay in their small cage, cramped and bored,
They can't help but think of their life before,
Roaming free, with their hopes high,
Can't they see the pain in their eyes?

Don't you think it's such a shame,
That us humans are the ones to blame?
The sadness, suffering and all the pain,
We're the monsters, and this needs to change.

Charlie Player (13)
Llanishen High School, Cardiff

There Are Certain Types Of Teachers

There are certain types of teachers.

A teacher parades through the classroom taking in the books, when he stops.
'Josh,' he cries, staring directly into the poor boy's eyes,
'Where is your book?' he enquires, then the boy answers coincidentally,
The professor bellows, not realising what problems he has.
He does not ask, he only shouts, he could have a reason,
He doesn't know whether he has lost it, if he is being bullied,
If there is trouble at home,
No, he just shouts.

She helps, she contributes, she's friendly,
But for the eyes of the robot-like minion, she is nobody
Though she is one of the best, the kindest, she is the same.

I wait as I ponder about the tall sixth former, sluggishly resting against the neighbour's wall.
I wait for my friend as another person strolls out of the gate,
I wait, still as this strange walks ahead, naive of the approaching sixth former,
Stepping, stepping, stepping forwards, the child is suddenly tugged by the collar,
He is brought closer to the sixth former who scolds the boy,
Then he kicks him, and beats him, as I pretend to unsee the event,

With no reminisce, a teacher comes out of the entrance, witnesses this happening and walks off,
With no care or attention for the younger child or me.

The gang waits 'round the back for its members,
It begins to circle the school grounds, bullying all unfortunate souls who pass,
Lesson starts as the rusted, iron bell clangs on its last legs and the gang is late,
While the gang differ to participate in any work, the boy tries his hardest, though he is being picked on,
Up and down goes his hand, and left and right goes his pen as he inscribes,
By the conclusion of the lesson, the gang has done near to nothing, while the boy's done all,
Yet the teacher, despite of this just thanks every one of them not praising some for participation, thinking *they are all the same.*

There are certain types of teachers:
There's the tedious tickers, who tick everything as the same, not admiring some of the effort,
There's the obnoxious overlookers, who don't ask questions and see things as they see, with no questions,
Furthermore, there's the unsatisfying samers, who think of their students as all the same
Additionally, there's the ignorant ignorers who pay no attention to the children in need,

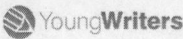

Then there's what the majority are:

All of the above

We are not the same, each of us are different with different interests, personalities, ideas, horizons and potentials.

To the robots and minions who are the teachers and the professors, don't just teach, *help!*

Matthew Hill (13)
Llanishen High School, Cardiff

What You Don't Know

It's what you don't know about the people around you
The people who are scared to stand in a queue
People who just cry for a reason you don't know
Who always have their books alphabetically in a row

We don't mean to have these weird panic attacks
It happens when the world gets scary and starts to turn
black
When my breathing goes crazy and it just won't stop
And a tear leaves my eye like a single raindrop

It's when my heart starts beating like a ticking clock
Some people try to help but others just mock
My head is screaming that it's about to explode
I don't know how to deal with an emotional load

I have been an extreme perfectionist all of my life
I don't always get things right and that leads to strife
Always worrying what people will think
It's a whirlpool of fear that never seems to shrink

Often I go tense when people try to touch me
My head is like a crashing, raging sea
That is too crazy for a small lifeboat to row
I tell you reader, it's the things you don't know.

Caitlin Preece (14)
Llanishen High School, Cardiff

You Don't Say Anything

It's easy to look at someone and not see the ugly
It's easy to compare your demons to their angels
It's easy to drown in the self doubt and anxiety
Because to pull yourself out of that state feels
almost impossible
So you don't say anything.

It's time like these that we never tell anyone
Because telling someone feels like a cry for help
And how is anyone supposed to help you
When the source of your tears seems indistinguishable?
How is anyone supposed to understand that one slight
mistake
Can cause a tsunami of vexation to hit?
It feels as if no one could ever comprehend
The amount of confusion that takes place in your mind
And you wouldn't be able to find the words
To try to explain to them
Even if you were given a script and
Three months in advance to practise
So you don't say anything.

You teach yourself to smile through it
Even if you can feel the adrenaline
Buzzing through your arms

And you can hear the spastic drum beat
In your ears
And your heart is a bird trapped in a cage, trying to escape
You don't say anything.

You might tie knots in your bobble
Or bounce your knee
In attempts to quieten your mind
Like finding things to fidget with
Will somehow satisfy the worry
We silence ourselves because we are taught that
Pain only exists if your arm is in a sling
Or if you're staggering from a limp
No one seems to pay attention
To the pain in your head
So you don't say anything.

But you wouldn't tell a dying man
To sit up and bear it
So why is it any different
When the illness is in your mind?
Because both can cause suffering
And ultimately
Both can take your life.

Darcy Kivell (14)
Llanishen High School, Cardiff

Why Is It Us?

Why is it us?
Why did we get letters saying we could no longer be one of
them?
Mother won't tell me, she says I won't understand.
All the other children look at me differently
And talk to each other in hushed voices if I'm around.
I tried to figure out what it was - my appearance?
Or perhaps the family business: selling feathers?
But the truth consumed me and I realised what it was.
It was because I was a Jew - and Hitler did not approve.

Why is it us?
Why is our cleaner here trying to warn us?
He has a picture of my father - Otto Billigheimer
- with a stamp underneath that says 'Dachau.'
I've heard the name 'Dachau' mentioned, but I'm not sure
what it is.
Father sent my sister and I upstairs to bed.
But I couldn't sleep,
Not with the cleaner's warning fresh in my mind.

Why is it us?
Why are we all of a sudden going to Switzerland on holiday?
We're being stopped in the airport and questioned about
trying to flee the country.
Why would we be doing that?

We eventually get through to Switzerland,
But mother says we won't be here long - we're moving to England.

Why is it us?
Why did we have to convert to Christianity?
The people here are much more friendly than in Munich.
I hear daily about the horrifying, cruel and malicious murders caused by Hitler;
Mine could've been one of them.
I'm finding it harder to learn English than Edith (my sister).
But still after all this time I only have one question.
Why is it us?

Sammy Wallington (13)
Llanishen High School, Cardiff

People Think

She walks down the corridor,
Pretending not to notice.
She says it's for the best,
They don't know she is broken.

You're gay, right?
Isn't that contagious?
He thinks he can say this,
To him it's not outrageous.

This happens every day
But no one seems to care
Or maybe they're just unaware
That people are suffering because of how they look.
Only because they like reading books,
Just because of their personality,
Even their sexuality.
Or the colour of their skin,
Some people wouldn't even begin to understand why that's wrong,
They think people who are different shouldn't belong.

She is sitting alone
Waiting for the bell,
Knowing the next day, she has to return
And pretend it's not Hell.

Whilst checking his Facebook
And seeing death threats are said
He thinks,
Wouldn't it be better if I were dead?

Do you think it's surprising?
That we all know a victim,
One of us could experience that severe criticism
But no one seems to care
No one does anything
We get told it's bad and it should stop
Yet there are thousands of people who still shed teardrops
Some people wouldn't even begin to understand why that's wrong,
They think people who are different shouldn't belong.

Caitlin King (13)
Llanishen High School, Cardiff

My Journey

Six unbearable, horrendous months
Six months of brutal combat,
Six months since I last spoke to my family,
Six months since I left Cardiff for Syria.

The relentless bombardment has rested in the house six
months feeling like six years
My job is to look out across the terrain and signal the sniper
below me
When any ISIS fighters have ventured across no-man's-land.
The sniper will fire and the outcome will be deadly.
That may sound easy to you but to me it's almost impossible
The bombing, the gunfire makes my job unbearable and I'm
powerless to stop it.
Cities, villages and towns all praying for the same outcome.
Peace.

Every day I wake to the deafening sound of gunfire as loud
as anything you could possibly imagine.
The screams bellowing from below me.
Every single time I hear the disturbing words, 'Man down.'
I think to myself, *what am I doing here? Why did I take the
risk to fight here?*
This is my life now. I made a choice, and I must do my duty
and save my country.

Six unbearable, horrendous months,
Six months of brutal combat,
Six months since I last spoke to my family,
Six months since I left Cardiff for Syria,
My journey is not coming to an end, it has only just begun.

Kieran Burns (13)
Llanishen High School, Cardiff

Slowly Breaking

The names, the jokes, the words,
Are knives through my soul.
Slowly breaking.

Are you happy now?
Now that I hate myself more than you?
Now that I cry every day after school?
I have nothing better to do,
I have no friends thanks to you.
The things you say replay across my mind,
Like a broken record.
My thoughts are consumed with nothing
but hatred for you, myself and everything.
My mind is whirring around,
Slowly breaking.

I starve myself so you won't call me fat,
I hide in make-up so you won't call me ugly,
I'll do anything for you to leave me alone,
But you won't.
You think it's funny to trip me in the hall?
You think it's cool to beat me up after school?
But do you think it's cool,
When you find me lying on the bathroom floor,
In a pool of blood?

Do you think it's funny?
You didn't kill me,
You destroyed me piece by piece,
My soul, my mind, my body.
I just did the dirty work for you.
Yet you still think it's not your fault,
And you've found a new kid,
To laugh at, to call names and to beat up.
But you don't know they're breaking inside,
Slowly breaking.

Olivia Camilleri (13)
Llanishen High School, Cardiff

It's Not Right

It's not right.
No trust, terrorism, racism.
It's not right.
Going out in the dark is as scary as a dog's bark.
It's not what it used to be,
Attacks happen left and right.
At the end of the day it's all a worthless fight.

Blackmail and mind games,
Why do they exist?
What's the point of interrogation?
Segregation still exists
I don't get it.

Blacks and whites they're different but they're the same,
Lungs, a heart, a brain, we all have one.
It's intelligence over the pigment of your skin.
Why do we judge others?
For pride, power and to be on top of a disturbing tower
I wonder what they would do if roles were reversed?
They wouldn't be smiling, they would be crying
And for good reason,
What they've done should be done for treason

Physical pain,
Captivity, mass murder, abuse
It's unnecessary.

Constantly fighting every day,
No one is peaceful anymore.
Where did it all go?

At this point global warming should be the only foe.
We can avoid it,
But we're not
It's not right.

Tommy Dafydd Barclay (13)
Llanishen High School, Cardiff

Welcome To High School

'Welcome to High School,' the first thing you said
When I moved to Year Seven,
Filled with ambition and hope for a future so bright,
I thought it was right but I was wrong.

Now I'm filled with the dread of the things in my head,
That won't let me sleep in the night.
My work's never done and there is no more fun,
Just the thoughts of writing in red.

Did I mention, the tension of the lesson
That's causing the depression of the next generation?
It's sweeping the nation.
The fear
The panic
I must get the homework in on time
The endless crime
The sentence is detention
There is no parole
It's taking its toll
A never-ending cycle of suppression.

Give us a break, how long will it take,
Before you realise the harm that you cause?
When the pressure for grades infects and invades!

Until there's nothing left of us
Just a cog in a machine
Wondering, whatever happened
To that big dream?

'Welcome to High School'
The first thing you said.
However you failed to mention
That my dreams would be dead.

Emma Navabi (13)
Llanishen High School, Cardiff

No Humanity

They're no longer human
Athletes controlled by coaches
Who feed on
Money, wealth and fortune.
Couldn't care less for their competitor's well being,
Not interested in their life
Outside sport.
They tried to revert,
Turn away,
But no,
Like animals the coaches
Keep forcing drugs into their clients
Making their humanity less than a human's should be
Reaping rewards but having so much
Athletes follow their masters blindly
Like hounds awaiting feeding.
No one warns them
No one cares,
No one sees the truth.
Athletes have become robotic entertainment
That are entirely obedient
To all orders.
The inhumanity.
The horror,
These drugs are ones of only misfortune and despair.

Only providing unneeded trouble
And capture for these dehumanised athletes
This isn't how it should be
These drugs abolished from existence
Returning the humanity into these blind athletes.
Drugs change everything.

Dylan Clayton
Llanishen High School, Cardiff

The Perfect Human Robot

Are we all just computerised?
Moulded into society?
Is the smile on our face just hiding the inside pain?
Scared to show our true colours, scared to show our true
feelings.
Forced into an unhealthy society, making ourselves fit in.
The boy feels hurt, feels pain, feels fear.
But inside school there is not one tear.
A smile computerised to get on with the day.
Computerised to keep the pain away.
Bang, bang, bang, the shots fire inside his head
'How's your day?' his happy mother said.

Poor as poor can be, was the boy,
Doesn't have the perfect hair, perfect name, perfect shoes,
perfect friends.
'Perfect, perfect, perfect,' shouted the voices inside his head.
'Perfect, perfect, perfect,' is what society says.
'You can't be different,' is what society says.
'You can't be you,' is what society says.

The human race is being changed every day.
The difference of others is being taken away.
A robot world may be the option,
Of a perfect human race selection.

Abby Francesca Tannetta (14)
Llanishen High School, Cardiff

They All Lie

Politicians may easily change policies to benefit their
influence and to increase their own reputation.
Nevertheless, when they see people struggling to get food
on the table
They turn a blind eye and move on.

They may say the peoples' interests are with them,
But the only thing they are about is the next big election,
Of their next big 'promise' is big enough,
Because at the end of the day countries should be run by a
democracy,
A fair and clear way of finding the next leader,
Not an autocracy or an aristocracy where everything
belongs to one,
But a way of rightly electing a leader in which we trust.

However, can we entirely trust this 'leader'?
With their promises and their claims to treat everyone the
same,
Yet singles out anyone that does not meet their set criteria,
Which in turn creates a mindset in people not to accept that
category of people.
In a world where leaders are from different countries,
religions and ethnicities,
They all have one thing in common.

They all lie.

Hamza Haddad (13)
Llanishen High School, Cardiff

Can You Hear Them Scream?

The world we live in can be cruel
Animals are tested against their will
Mice, birds, reptiles and others too
Locked in cages feeling blue

The kind of pain and suffering they endure
From needles, blood-tests and infections galore
Sore eyes and inflamed skin
92% of these tests end up in the bin

Would they put humans through this ordeal?
Do they know how the test subjects really feel?
Assessing drugs, cosmetics and medicines to name a few
Infestations, poisoning, skin-loss and death ensue

Some examples of animal abuse that we know
Include jabbing and poking them from head to toe
Killing pregnant animals stooping so low
Is this a fair outcome? The answer is NO

Animals cannot talk but have rights too
We need people to fight for them - how about you?
Pressure in the media and from organisations over time
May achieve some changes for animals down the line

People campaign and people do try
But no one breaks through the big lie

Emma Catherine Walker (13)
Llanishen High School, Cardiff

Who Is To Blame?

A production line of people,
Who are all made to look the same,
People we are expected to be,
To society this is no game.

One girl stares in the mirror,
She stands there wondering why,
Why is she not a model?
Why is there no gap in-between her thighs?

Then there's a boy, stood in his room,
No matter how hard he tries,
He is still questioning himself,
Why can't he be strong like so many other guys?

So the girl starts to starve,
She thinks there's nothing wrong, that isn't right,
All her family can do is stare,
Stare at such a frightful sight.

The boy starts to get into drugs,
Anything he can get his hands on to make him strong,
However none of his family or friends know,
Is it the boy or society at wrong?

To impressionable people this is no game,
They all must have the same profile,
Any route to get there they will take,
Even if the route is awfully vile.

Sophia Mohammed (13)
Llanishen High School, Cardiff

Poem

It starts with a beginning, like most things do,
But this one's a little bit strange.
It has rhythm, repetition and rhyme in there too,
And techniques of a wide range.

The beginning is short, but here's the fun part,
When the reader is really engaged.
The middle, the section that comes from the heart,
Where the techniques come out of their cage.

It's when words come crawling out of the page,
And create images of any kind.
The images could be joyful or filled with rage,
And that's just in your mind.

You carry on reading, you just can't stop,
Your eyes like cars with no brakes.
The rhyme is consistent from bottom to top,
Like the texture of bread that you bake.

The end of the poem is finally here,
You knew it had to come soon.
It's come off the paper and it's stuck in your ear,
You'll recite it from morning to noon.

Benjamin Davies (13)
Llanishen High School, Cardiff

Stereotypes

We're not the same,
We're different,
We've got different figures, feelings and names,
But...
We're perfect in our own way.

How many times do you look in the mirror?
Once, twice, three times, more like 50,
Trust me it's never going to make you thinner.

We should stop with labels,
Like thin, fat, short, tall,
There's just too many expectations.

We're not going to look like models,
With thigh gaps, perfect teeth, hair and shape.
We're not put on production lines like bottles.

If we were the same we would be boring,
And we would most certainly die out,
And that's a warning,

So love yourself for what's on the inside,
After all the outside is just a shell,
And remember there is no guide.

It's just you!

Caitlyn Boyle (13)
Llanishen High School, Cardiff

The Bullies

'Hey, hey you.'
They say as you're walking to the rusted gate
Worried about what they are going to say.
The people who pick on you call you names
And make fun of your parents too.

Well, you know what? Nobody cares.
Ignore them because they are only trying to bring you down
Because you are above them.
You're better.
They are nothing to you.
You know why?
Because they are bullies.

Every day is the same for them, come to school, bully, go
home.
But wait... not this time, not today
Because you've got the world on your side.
You've got your mum, your dad, your favourite teacher, your
least favourite teacher
And even your next door neighbour's uncle's cat.
All that they've got is a bad attitude.
Take that away and they're just like the rest.

Alex Criddle (13)
Llanishen High School, Cardiff

People Aren't As They Seem

People aren't as they seem
Not all have high self-esteem
Not all are happy and content
Only ten percent seek help
Stop trying to be like Kendall and Kylie
Stop trying to make yourself skinny.

People aren't as they seem
You can't see what's underneath
At school they may be confident and sure
At home they are feeling so much more.

People aren't as they seem
You may think they're the dream
You may think they're beautiful
But their mirror may say unsuitable
You think, how are they so perfect?
But you really don't inspect them

People aren't as they seem
On the inside, you may want to scream
Not because you may have low self-esteem
You don't realise you're an *amazing moonbeam!*

Isabelle Coutts (13)
Llanishen High School, Cardiff

This Is What I Call Home!

Cramped, isolated, enclosed
This is what I call home!
I have nowhere to go
And nowhere to play.
While I am being stared
And pointed at throughout the day.
Cramped, isolated, enclosed,
Do you call this home?

Moving in small circles,
Like a dog chasing its tail.
Day becomes night
Then night becomes day.
Each day passing,
In exactly the same way.
Cramped, isolated, enclosed,
Do you call this home?

Separated from family,
At a young age.
Still sitting here in isolation,
Being made to entertain.

As I swing from the arching branches,
With the cameras in my face.
I moan my objections
About living in this place.
Cramped, isolated, enclosed,
Do you call this home?

Lewis Vaughan (13)
Llanishen High School, Cardiff

Different Yet The Same

White, black or brown
We are all human.
Gay, lesbian, bisexual or straight
We are all human.
Christian, Jewish, Hindu or Muslim
We are all human.
We are all equal.
We all have rights.
So when a person or a group of people are singled out
because of what they feel or believe in,
I ask myself, why?
We are all entitled to our own belief
So, why?
Why can't we accept that we are all equal, no one is more
important than the other?
Why can't we accept that we are all different, and that
difference is good?
Who put a man before a woman?
Who said one skin colour should be superior to the other?
No matter our differences, ultimately we are the same.
Ultimately we are one.
Ultimately we are one race.
Ultimately, we are human.

Thomas Jonathan Davies (14)
Llanishen High School, Cardiff

The These And Those

People call people fat.
Yet these people who call those people fat
Have no right to say that.
Because when these people call those people fat,
Those people will look in the mirror
And start worrying what they're really looking at.
Then these people call people skinny,
Then those people who get called that
Then start to panic about why that he or she might describe
her ribs as the same as a stray cat's.
Because when these people call those people this,
Those people don't think about the effect
That these people get when those people say these things
with a slight hiss.
So when you ever think about calling those people skinny or
fat,
Think about what they might think of you or themselves
Once you've said something like that.

Emily Cann (14)
Llanishen High School, Cardiff

Bullying

I keep to myself
I don't bother anyone
I do my work in class.
I'm not late to class or school.
So why do they call me names?
Why do they push me?
Why me?

Should I put up with this?
Bang! My ears ring as I hit the ground.
Everyone laughs.
They laugh.
No one helps as they kick me.
Not even the teachers.
I'm on my own.
Why me?

I've had enough.
I'm going to fight back.
They go to hit me but I hit first.
Silence as he hits the ground.
They back off.
I hear a teacher
'You!' he screams. 'Get here!'
It's my fault for fighting back.
But no one listens to those who need it the most.
Why me?

Cory Ford (13)
Llanishen High School, Cardiff

What Do You See?

When you stand in front of the mirror,
What do you see?
Do you see yourself or what you should be?
Should you be taller?
Should you be skinnier?
Should your nose be straighter?
Should your tummy be smaller?

When you stand in front of the mirror,
What do you see?
Do you see yourself or what you could be?
Could you be stronger?
Could you be richer?
Could you be better?
Could you be happier?

When you stand in front of the mirror,
What do you see?
Do you see yourself or what you would be?
Would you be more satisfied?
Would you be more popular?
Would you be more confident?
Would you be more sociable?

When I look in the mirror I see me!

Harriet Beattie (13)
Llanishen High School, Cardiff

War

The cold feel of a fray grenade in your hand,
Lobbing it to the enemy's trench.
The firing of assault rifles filled the battlefield,
The screeching of master shells falling from the gloomy sky.
Crimson trails led to the fallen like magma from a volcano.

The shouts and screams of injured comrades,
Echoed through your war-filled mind.
The engines of tanks roared
Jets blasting through the sky.
A bright flash of a sniper lining up the shot
The firing of guns giving suppressive fire.

A grenade is lobbed at you and time freezes
Your life flashed before you.
A thundering boom
Ringing in ears.
You're bleeding out.

Joshua Smith (14)
Llanishen High School, Cardiff

War Never Changes

One by one my comrades fall,
Bullets coming in from all angles,
How many more deaths before this war ends?
I've lost many allies and friends,
War, war never changes.

My knees are weak,
My arms are heavy,
I push up to the beach,
My gun at the ready,
Even more of my allies fall,
And if I have learnt one thing,
It's that war, war never changes.

It's the final assault,
The few of my allies remaining,
They shout a warning,
And in a split second,
It all changes.
From one explosion,
Our lives end,
War, war never changes.

Thomas Lamb (13)
Llanishen High School, Cardiff

All I Ask Is For You To Campaign

They imported me here by plane,
And leave me alone in the rain,
How do they not feel any shame,
For all this pointless pain?
All I ask is for you to campaign.

The forest is my domain,
Not being restrained here by a chain,
While they whip me with a cane,
Sometimes I wonder if humans have a brain,
All I ask is for you to campaign.

They can starve me again
Because I refuse to entertain,
I want to roam free on my own terrain,
This place is driving me insane,
All I ask if for you to campaign.

Alfie Sewell (13)
Llanishen High School, Cardiff

Equality

It's OK to be different,
It's OK to be you,
We should all be treated the same,
No one treated different,
All of us,
The same,
Yes of course we are different in some ways,
Short hair,
Long hair,
Tall people,
Short people,
Brown eyes,
Blue eyes,
But no black person should be told to get out,
Because of the colour of their skin
No white person should be told no,
Because of the colour of their skin,
We are all human
We are all different
But never stop being you.

Lauren May Thompson (13)
Llanishen High School, Cardiff

Equality

Bullying, it's everywhere
In school, at home, in work
You shouldn't be bullied for being you
Everyone is different
No matter what size, shape look, religion you are
We are all different
Don't be afraid to be who you are
We are all human
Black, white
White, black
No human should be told no because of their colour skin
No human should be ignored
Because of their colour skin
We are all different
Don't bully people because they're different.

Anna Rose Borley (13)
Llanishen High School, Cardiff

Hate Crimes

It feels like Brexit is the only exit
And all the chatter about them not selling fish batter
Is just tatter
Because the real matter is the hate crime attacks
As the racist whacks the immigrant
As they come imminent as the refugee locks his door.
He's going to attack because he does not have what they have
So he feels like the immigrant stole it.
The teacher stands in the back as he assaults the preacher
Because he does not want him in his country.

George John (13)
Llanishen High School, Cardiff

Sport

Step by step, pass by pass,
Sport clears your mind for the day ahead,
For the passion of the game,
No matter what was said,
Do it for the love not the money,
Do it for your teammates,
Do whatever it takes to succeed,
All leading up to the final strand,
You have to work hard, we've agreed,
The roar of the crowd in the stand,
Hours of training,
There can't be complaining
That's sport!

Tom Bridge (13)
Llanishen High School, Cardiff

Regret

I've committed a sin
Now the trouble begins.
The sirens start screeching
The law begins reaching.
They're out for their vengeance
Now I'm feeling repentant.

I've committed a sin.
Oh what trouble I'm in.
What was I thinking.
That night I went drinking.

I've committed a sin.
I feel regret from within.
In a moment of fury
I now face the jury.

Callum Porteous (13)
Llanishen High School, Cardiff

Change For Equality

Should we be treated equally
And have the right to live peacefully
Or should there be war?

Should we all be the same,
Or is being different to blame
For all the problems in the world?

Can this be sorted?
Will people be supported
In changing the world?

If everyone had a say,
Would the world be this way?
Maybe then it would be fair.

Kim Emily Brown (13)
Llanishen High School, Cardiff

Black, White Divide

We're no longer living in 1963,
All different races should be free.
Free to be themselves,
Not to be put in a certain place,
Just to be free living whatever their race.
Whether you're black or white,
You shouldn't have to fight.
Fight for your freedom,
Fight for your rights.

Anna Jenkins Delf (13)
Llanishen High School, Cardiff

Friendship

Friendship is like the colours of the rainbow,
Always in sight wherever you go

Red like an apple, sweet to the core,
Once you have one you're always waiting for more

Orange like a burning flame, never dying out,
But always the same

Yellow like the sun that brightens our day,
It touches the heart of everyone, with its beautiful rays

Green like a plant that keeps on growing,
its leaves reaching out wherever I'm going

Blue like the water that is so pure,
Wherever it is headed, it knows for sure.

Purple like a flower that is ready to bloom,
In my heart, it always has room.

Sometimes the rainbow can spring some,
Clouds means bullies and some clowns
If you see a rainbow, smile
Because sometimes you miss a chance
To be a part of a rainbow.

Jade Evans
Pencoed Comprehensive School, Bridgend

Penguins Of The World

Penguins are smart
Penguins are cute
They remind me of men in waiters' suits
With long, black coats and white, buttoned shirts
Waddling about, always happy to serve

Penguins are smart
Penguins are cute
The Rock Hopper with its funny yellow hair
Jumps about almost everywhere
Riding the surf with their pals by their side
Arriving at shore on their bellies they glide

Penguins are smart
Penguins are cute
The African penguin all slender and sleek,
Walking, sliding, oh watch how they leap
Into the air like a plane as they go then swiftly
Nose-diving back into the snow

Penguins are smart
Penguins are cute
There's seventeen species and to name just a few
Emperor, King and Adelie all in a queue
So look them all up they are waiting for you.

Thomas Lloyd Freeman-Jones (12)

Pencoed Comprehensive School, Bridgend

My School Day

When the clock strikes six
And all I smell is Mum making cake mix.
It's time to jump out of bed,
And stop being a lazy head.
My tie goes up high,
And all that's left to do is say goodbye.
I jump to the door,
And that's when the day becomes a chore.
I arrive at school
And see the teacher being cruel
I try to act cool
But realise I only look a fool.
The days are always a bore
It's even harder when it pours.
When the clock strikes quarter past three,
I leave the school gate flying like a bee.
I arrive home,
And lie in my bed like a gnome.
The school day is over,
And my face smiles like a clover.
I say goodnight,
And wait for my alarm to shine bright.

Nakita Mayle
Pencoed Comprehensive School, Bridgend

Friends

Short or tall it doesn't matter at all.
No matter their name,
No two friends are the same.
Some are caring,
Some are daring,
Some are scary, some are weary.
No matter what they say or do,
Friends are always there for you.
Black or white,
Round or light,
You may fight,
But friends stick together forever.
Friends aren't made in factories,
They can't all be the same.
That doesn't mean that you should shout,
Or place them for the blame.
My friends are always there for me,
No matter, day or night.
If I need them,
They'll be there,
As fast as the speed of light.
Friends stick together forever.

Molly Harris
Pencoed Comprehensive School, Bridgend

Untitled

A schoolboy holds a leather ball in a photograph on his
bedroom wall
The bed is made, curtains drawn at the silence in the break
of dawn
A football kit folded neatly lies beneath his feet
This should have been a special time for a boy who would
be in his prime
Everyone remembers that day when he walked through the
door
They have had too much time to adore, leaving us wanting
more
As the game got underway, there were shouts from the
crowd of disarray
The pleas and cries, the screams for help
The screams from that day
His outstretched arms then despair, the highest 27 years of
tears
As the souls of those who fell, await the toll of the justice
bell
He will 'Never Walk Alone'.

Bradley David John Withers (12)

Pencoed Comprehensive School, Bridgend

Love Is Love

Black and white,
Can't you see between the lines?
Gay or lesbian,
Why does that matter?
Asian or European
We're all different.
Big or small
Everyone is unique in their own way.
As quiet as a mouse
Or as loud as a firework,
They're just labels,
Labels that don't actually matter.
Mother and Father,
Or Mother and Mother
Or Father and Father,
They're still family,
Why are people taking that away?
Times have changed,
But love is still love,
No matter what age,
No matter what ethnic group,
No matter what gender.
Love is love
Who it's between shouldn't matter.

Kira Paul
Pencoed Comprehensive School, Bridgend

My Star

Written for my dad who passed away in 2009.

I look to the sky to see if you are there
You are so far away but I know you are near
The twinkling glow that lights the night
You are the thing that makes my life bright.

I miss the way we play
The way you hugged me every day
Your voice has gone and I can't see
But I'm sure you are there watching down on me.

Losing you I was in such a bad way
I miss and think of you every single day
The star that shines doesn't make me feel so bad
I'm proud that you were my special dad.

Morgan Poole (13)
Pencoed Comprehensive School, Bridgend

Rich

My mother says that,
Money doesn't grow on trees,
Trees are Mother Nature,
But in my world they're money makers,
Mom's trees sway in the garden,
But in my world money flies everywhere,
The park's trees sway in the fields,
But my world money flies everywhere,
The school's trees sway in the playground,
But in my world money flies everywhere,
Money is wonderful things,
I wish they'd grow some wings,
If I sit tight and keep calm,
I hope it will just fly into my palm.

Jack Morris
Pencoed Comprehensive School, Bridgend

Football

Football is a beautiful game;
I play it every day even in the rain.

I love playing football, it keeps me fit,
I could play it forever and never quit.

I really want our team to score
And I love it when we win,
But when it's over
I want to play some more!

Even though we can't win every game
The coach wants us to have fun,
It doesn't matter if we win or lose
Our team is still number one.

Roan Burnett
Pencoed Comprehensive School, Bridgend

Alfie

A is for amazing, he goes through so much you see
L is for the laughter that he brings to you and me
F is for the fear and pain that he feels
I is the inspiration he is to everyone he meets
E is the envy I'm sure you all feel, 'cause Alfie's my brother
and we're keeping it real.

I think he's fantastic,
He really is great,
He's my little brother,
My very special mate.

Ellis Jones (12)

Pencoed Comprehensive School, Bridgend

Four Leaf Clover

A four leaf clover
They are very rare
Maybe a bit like us
None of us are bare
Because we are all rare
No one's like each other.

A four leaf clover
If we ever find one
Always keep it
Cherish it
Love it
Like we are all the same
Yes we may look different
But really we are very alike

Four leaf clover
Are so very rare
A bit like us then.

Georgina Austin
Pencoed Comprehensive School, Bridgend

Christmas

C hildren tucked away sleeping
H omes warm with the fires burning
R eindeer flying into the night
I cicles dripping down the roof
S anta delivering all the toys
T oys waiting for the kids to wake up
M istletoe dangling from the ceiling
A ngels upon the Christmas tree
S now falling onto the ground.

Taine Josif Evans (12)
Pencoed Comprehensive School, Bridgend

Rock On

I listen to rock music loud
And it makes me feel happy and proud
I like the beat of the drum
And I love the sound of the guitar as it starts to strum
My headache throbs when I listen to pop
I scream at the radio, 'Make it stop!'
Bring on the bands Stereophonics and Green Day
They are the bands that inspired me to play
Rock on!

Ioan Whittington (12)
Pencoed Comprehensive School, Bridgend

Rugby

Aggressive tackles
Fired up coaches ready to go
Nervous players wait

Set blitz defence to
Stop thundering Lions centre
Gibbs tramples the Ox

Massive players clash
George North and Israel Folau
Lion tames Wallaby.

Llŷr Aeron Harries (12)
Pencoed Comprehensive School, Bridgend

The Fairy Godmother

A blanket lay over far far away
As the fairy godmother flew.
A blanket of complete tranquillity
Or so she thought she knew.

A shriek filled the cold night air
And she darted to the sound
Only to find a young servant girl
Sitting on the ground.

'My life is a mess!' the poor girl cried,
'I can't go to the Ball!
There is nothing in this life for me,
Nothing good at all!'

'My dear what's wrong?' the fairy asked
Wanting to try and help.
'I'm sure I could be of some aid to you,
Just please don't cry and yelp!'

'You're the fairy godmother!' she gasped,
Her eyes filled with wonder.
'I've heard that you grant wishes for people,
Can you make me look ten years younger?

And how about a big ball gown,
With glass slippers to match?
With your help I'll be stunning,
A prince I'm sure to catch!'

The fairy godmother stood and watched
The girl demand her list,
She was sure everyone else in the country,
Only got one wish!

'A carriage I want, two footmen too,
And my hair done up in a bun.
Come on old lady, let's not waste time,
We are nowhere near done!'

So the fairy did as she was asked,
Or more accurately - told!
She waved her wand over the girl
And let her magic unfold...

She changed the girl's rags into a gown
Of blue, with golden jewelled lacing.
Then set out to find two mice for footmen,
Which she took an hour chasing!

Next she found two more to be horses
And a pumpkin for a carriage.
She found herself pitying the poor man
Who would be forced into this marriage!

After the fairy had completed the list
She decided to play a trick.
A trick to teach the girl a lesson
When she heard a grand clock tick...

'Enjoy the ball but be aware,
There's a limit on the time.
Twelve o'clock is when everything goes
Because the shoes you're wearing are mine!'

Then she flew away back into the night
While everything was hushed
She knew the girl would never marry
If everything was rushed!

Holly Tee (12)
St Illtyd's Catholic High School, Cardiff

Autumn

Autumn is great,
Hot chocolate on the way.
Stepping on leaves,
Stepping in puddles,
New lives for lambs,
Running around fields and playing.

When I think of autumn I think of new lives,
When I think of autumn I think leaves falling off trees,

When autumn comes nature comes,
Birds chirping in the trees, in the forests,
People walking through forests.

Children playing in the park,
People walking their dogs through fields,
More flowers been planted and growing,

More bugs coming, bees buzzing around,
Children picking the flowers from fields and gardens,
Playing with mates in parks,
Kids going to school,
Going for walks.

When I think of autumn I think of kids playing in the park,
When I think of autumn I think of kids drinking hot
chocolate,
When I think of autumn I think of bugs,
When I think of autumn I think of flowers.

Kaitlyn Davies (13)
Ysgol Aberconwy, Conwy

First World Problems

The wifi's gone for the millionth time today
It's raining,
I press my face against the window
And watch the raindrops
Slowly at first
Just a splitter-splatter on the pavement
Then faster
More and more lonely little drops of water
Until they're coming down like an army
Like they've declared war
And all of a sudden I think
I wonder why?
Why they let such idiots run our country
Why I bother to vote
Why the toaster is broken
And the neighbours have woken
And are arguing again?

My bones sigh with fatigue for the millionth time today
As I traipse home
Along the dusty, dirty orange-grey of a road
The weight of the school books under my arm
The heat of the fierce sun
My guilt at leaving my sister at home
It weighs heavy on me
My stomach growls with hunger
But I remember how lucky I am

I go to school
I get up at 5am
Not to fetch water or face being married off
But to an education.
Education?
That means a future
A hope away from eternal poverty
A hope of waking up to more
Than an empty stomach.

One day I'll get a promotion
It's stopped raining now
Still I sit by the window and contemplate
One day I'll see a bigger house
In a bigger neighbourhood
My wifi will work
And life will be good.

One day I'll have a job
It's past 5pm now
The sun's intense heat is fading
Still I trudge home
And think
One day I'll leave school
I'll get a job
I'll start a family
I'll bring up a child in a world

Where they don't know what hungry feels like
Where they can have clean water
And two pairs of shoes
And life will be good.

Ruth Dean (15)
Ysgol Aberconwy, Conwy

Untitled

Thousands dead, society destroyed -
All because of religion they said.
Muslims forever hidden in the shadow of terrorism,
As more continue to believe what they're told.

Sheep - the lot of them constantly
Taunting, humiliating those that are blamed.
Why? Why judge an entire religion
Just because of the small majority of them that don't follow
the rules?
Why choose to believe those that twist the truth?
Do you not have a mind of your own?

It's all a lie. All of it,
Yes it's tragic what's happened.
Yes it's devastating how many innocent people have lost
their lives.
But religion isn't always the problem,
And yet still every minute of every hour the deadly,
controlling darkness
Begins to spread more and more,
And nothing can stop it.

Don't discriminate. don't judge,
Just because they say it's true,
Doesn't mean it is.

Aiden James Jones (15)
Ysgol Aberconwy, Conwy

Say No

Say no
That's a command Officer Girl Child of the millennial
Millenia
Millennium.
Over population, starvation, life advice, heart is a vice
Pens, pencils, rubber and a ruler.
Simply don't let them sweat it.
Education reform
We can be reborn, less blind to reality.
Fingers through your hair, born naked and afraid
Third World
First World,
For First world... girl child... too vile.
It's your opinion, your decision... you decide your destiny?
Adolescent ladies, eradication of unnecessary mutilation
against... the will of the girl child
You're opinionated and trashy, not classy...
Here we go again.
Conservative or socialist,
Motionless or emotionless,
Floater or dead set voter.
Rope her... dote her...
Set free our dreams of owning a home
And growing alone without a child or tradition.
Keep it... don't sweep it.
Let me play for slightly longer.

Let me move to the city let me say no and...
Just let me go... life experience? Stuff that, I own it, it's me.
Girl child of the 21st century at your service.
It's scary to think of the statistics.
Unconfirm it, don't just accept it.
Unfree the freedom of being wed at just ten...
By a man you met yesterday, can't comprehend in your head.
Right to legal care, but formation says no.
Legal cane and protection from...
Violence
And discrimination.
Innovating
Empowering
Victimised...
For being victimised.
Against the thrill
The thrill...
That never belongs to the girl child
That never belongs to us...
That never belongs to...
Me.

Ffion Harrison-Boothby (15)
Ysgol Aberconwy, Conwy

Wales

Wales is what this poem's about,
From castles to mountains to Brussels sprouts,
The country with the mighty red dragon is the best by far,
You can get there by plane, on a ship or car.

In Wales there's mountains, sea and sky,
You can watch through your window and see birds fly,
There's hot weather and cold weather, you can never tell,
But there's always something to cheer you up or make you feel well.

The Welshmen have also been to France
To play some football, you must have heard or maybe seen them dance
The atmosphere was so, so loud,
Wales were so, so proud

If you think of Wales, you may think of just flowers,
But if you ask me about Wales, we could be here for hours.
Without this lovely country we wouldn't have the scone,
So that's another good reason to come along.

You could buy some lovely Welsh lamb or meat,
It's gorgeous and fresh, go have a treat,
Farming in Wales is a very large passion,
And one thing's for sure, it won't go out of fashion.

Wherever you go there's something to do,
For the north to the south there's attractions to view,
Climb up Snowdon or ride the zip wire,
And visit the Great Orme for views to admire,

Wales is beautiful you've got to believe,
Once you arrive you won't want to leave,
So come on over and visit us here,
Everywhere's open all through the year!

Aron Jones (11)
Ysgol Aberconwy, Conwy

Pressure

So...
Drugs stink
They make you stink and even worse
They kill
Kill, smell and illegal,
Drugs are negative towards everything.
They're absolutely awful.
People on drugs think they're cool
But,
They're just cruel.
When they go to bed
They're most likely to wake up
Dead.
It's nobody's fault except themselves
So
Never feel sorry for them.
Don't ever use drugs
Unless you want
Your teeth to rot,
Your breath to stink,
Your clothes to stink,
Your body to look disgusting
And
To be in terrible pain,
Use your sense
And stay away from drugs.

Let drugs kill themselves,
It looks like people like doing it
But they don't
They are just addicted!
If it's not cool then
Why do people do it?
People do it because
They think
They look like the big ones
Doing drugs
But no they definitely don't
People should know better than to
Throw your only life
Away like it's a plastic bag
So...
Use all of
The sense that you have got in your brain
And...
Stay away from drugs.
If you see a needle
Just ignore it
And walk away
But
Make sure to tell a parent
Because it's serious
Leave drugs alone.

Hopefully that has taught people to stay away
Because drugs
Are
Too serious.

James Todd (12)
Ysgol Aberconwy, Conwy

The Bullies Are About

It's happening at any time
At any given place
So in this little, tiny rhyme
I'll tell it to your face

Bullies taking over the school
Big, bad and mean
They think they are so fit to rule
And us their breakfast's beans

We always try to stop them
But they laugh and pull our hair
Then when the teachers come to check
They're straight out of there!

If we talk to any staff
Or even mention their name
They'll find you in lessons like maths
And continue with their game

This problem needs to be solved
Bullies will be no more
They really need to be dissolved
We'll rock them to their core

Thank you for listening!
And remember to watch out
Just don't, don't do anything stupid
The bullies are about!

Malin Owen (12)

Ysgol Aberconwy, Conwy

My Hero

This is about my hero, she is funny, smart and kind,
She helps me with the choices I make,
she always has the time.
My hero helps me with my homework and listens to me read
My hero is a patient soul, she is all I ever need.
When I am good or bad, happy or sad,
she is always by my side,
Supporting and encouraging me, my ever helpful guide.
On manners, school and homework
she will not stand for 'No,'
She teaches me what's right from wrong
and encourages me to grow.
My hero smiles at me and makes my heart sing,
She truly is my earth angel, just without the wings.
My hero loves me unconditionally in each and every way,
She strives to give me confidence
to help me through my day.
My hero is always there, my respect for her is immense
Being with her is where I want to be,
there's never a pretence.
My hero's hair is dyed blonde,
her eyes are brown and glisten,
Her face is kind without a frown
and when I speak she listens.

My hero is my grandmother,
a fact I am sure you had guessed
A grandmother's love is special
and I really feel I am blessed.

Ruby Rose Rinaldi (11)
Ysgol Aberconwy, Conwy

Sweet Shop Selection

Sweets line the shelves,
All for the taking. We ignore
The ones we have,
And we pick our favourites.

People line by the sour sweets,
We avoid those.
Instead we find the sweet, sugary treats,
The ones we tend to favour.
And so we get used to the sweet,
And never try an alternative.

But sometimes a sweet is disguised,
As something it isn't
A lollipop for example
The appearance looks sweet. It's centre isn't
Or a bonbon, the outside looks rough,
But it's heavenly sweet just inside.

Should we try something new?
But we, as people, do not like change,
We stick to what we know. What we like.
And we refuse to change.

'Cariad, would you like a sour ball?' a lady at the till asks.
We refuse, we don't like change.

Although, people can change,
People change all the time.
Last week you liked sour sweets,
Next week I could like them again.

Now as you walk past another old sweet shop,
You pause and think
'Do I try something new?'

Charlotte Stevenson (15)
Ysgol Aberconwy, Conwy

Earth's Changing

The Earth is getting hot
And crumbling
To bits, one day it might not be there,
Floods that could kill cities and towns.
Make them fall to the ground, if we keep going like this.
It won't be here for longer.
If you recycle you are helping the world to stay healthy,
More people help the longer we're here.

If you pollute the world
You're not helping yourself.
Factory and cars destroying the ozone layer,
When it breaks that is it.
It's gone forever,
It's not coming back ever.
The seas would rise, flood towns,
Would kill wildlife.
Would kill eco-systems
Would kill us in the end.

If you walk instead of taking the car, you're helping.
If we all do do that,
It will help us all.
Factories stop burning rubbish, we will be here longer.

We are cutting forests down, getting rid of wildlife.
We need plants to live, to make oxygen, to stay alive.
Do you want this to happen?
Think about it.

David Lewis (14)
Ysgol Aberconwy, Conwy

Drugs

Drugs need to stop now!
Quicker than ever
If not the world is finished.
Drugs have to stop,
It is increasing death
But if needed it's okay,
If it will help you live.

Drugs need to stop now!
If not, it is like shooting a bow and arrow
At someone's head
But it's not,
It's just me trying to persuade people to not take drugs,
Just take care of yourself and please
Never ever take drugs again!

If drugs don't stop,
The population of the world will go lower each year.
The question for the world is,
Is the world ever going to be happy again?

I don't want to see any more sad stories about drugs
Because it is a huge headache.
It is just not ideal to take drugs,
So for the last time please stop drugs to be out of this world,
So don't take them because you are teasing us in a bad way.

All I want to do is persuade the world to stop taking drugs
That is all I can ask for!
Just pray drugs to be out of this world for good.

Ben Ahari (12)
Ysgol Aberconwy, Conwy

Global Warming

Why litter?
Why cut the trees?
Why graffiti?
Will global warming happen?
Why should we let it happen?
So let's start by doing, making the world a better place.
We need to learn to:
Love
Share
And don't litter anymore
Don't graffiti anymore on the wall.
But the world is still living on a dirty world that never
could be fixed.
Just please stop
Stop
Stop
Please just stop and think what you are about to do.
Just
Stop
Stop
And listen to people when they say, 'Put it in the bin.'
Think about the animals in the woods
They can die of:
Glass
Plastic
Poison food/bad food.

They can really get hurt.
So stop!
Global warming can happen if you let it.
The sun can disappear if you carry on
Just
No
No
Earth is going to stop and we won't be alive.

Amy Davis (12)
Ysgol Aberconwy, Conwy

Untitled

Still silence filled with the warmth of your body
Radiating on me while we sleep
I wouldn't dream of being anywhere else other than lying
next to you.

The light is just dim enough that I can see
The smile you give me after we kiss goodnight,
I can't sleep, I can't dream if I can't have you.

There's a demon inside me,
He is called Anxiety,
He shouts and screams,
Until I can barely breathe,
He makes me feel sick,
Weak in my knees,
Oh please Mr Anxiety
Just let me be.

The rustle of sheets
The pacing of feet
And the lights outside flicker in the dark street
That is covered in sleet
The house is losing heat
Shiver under blankets
To gain warmth is a feat

When the big hands meets
The little hand, there are seats
That are inanimate and cold
Anxiety ain't sweet.

Ashleigh Hughes (12)

Ysgol Aberconwy, Conwy

Countryside

Close your eyes, imagine yourself on a hill
Birds flying past your head
The wind rustling the leaves in the trees.

The setting sun shining
Through the golden trees
The red, white and yellow flowers
The grass waving from side to side.

Now close your eyes
Can I hear it?
That sound close now
Can you bear it?
Open your eyes see it?
War and fire burning everything

Lives torn apart day by day
World War One? The war to end all wars
World War Two? The biggest human conflict.

Cavemen didn't start wars
They were still vicious
But still ambitious
They laid the foundation for inventions
How did we use these inventions?
Guns, bombs, nukes, tanks

Don't be proud we won a war
Be sad
Be mad
You don't remember those who lost their lives do you?

Daniel Roberts (14)

Ysgol Aberconwy, Conwy

Bullying

Bullying is wrong,
It's so mean,
Bullying can go too far,
It's really bad, it's worse than it seems,
Hiding from the truth a bully's victim bleeds
Stop bullying now it doesn't make you cool,
In front of your friends it's not funny at all
Bad bully, why do you do it?
It's not nice, it's nasty and spite.
Naughty, nasty not nice at all.
Pick someone your own size,
Bullies think they stand tall, however,
Sometimes bullying is breaking the law.
Be careful what you wish for,
At least try to be nice
Or after mucky phone calls, hear a knock on your door.
Sorry to people who suffer from this pain
However, bullies can change their hearts and
Think like they're sane.

Violet Holly Paton (11)
Ysgol Aberconwy, Conwy

And Again

I was so close, yet so exceedingly far.
I wanted to run.
I was already running
His grasp would catch me, and he would have me.
Then I would be his...
His words would torture me, so much so
'Get someone you love.' 'Get someone you need!'
The irony -
He smiled his ever so gruesome smile,
As he proceeded to take what was left of me.

This was demonic. God didn't ask for this.
Although is there really a God?

He spun me around, like a dancer doing a pirouette,
But not at all gracefully.
I was face to face with his soulless, pebbled eyes.
Was darkness actually this dark?
I had associated such a colour with grief, loneliness,
isolation...
Emptiness.
Normality, normality doesn't make it,
Normal

And again.

Tegan Haf Simpson (14)
Ysgol Aberconwy, Conwy

Stop Bullying

Bullies beat you,
Bullying online and in school,
People calling you names
Ugly, fat, skinny, tall, small
These words can mean much more!

Too scared to stand up to them,
They're stronger than me, taller than me,
They shout, drag me out on the yard,
They hit me and kick me,
Throwing me around,
They shout louder, louder.

Hitting, punching every day,
Scared to tell my mum what happened today!
But what happens at home didn't help me at all,
All the shouting at home,
The noises all around me.

All I want to do is learn at school,
Not get hit and punched,
I want to go to school happy!
I want to go home happy!
Stop bullying!
What have people done to get bullied all the time?

Just stop bullying.

Lydia Smith (12)
Ysgol Aberconwy, Conwy

Machines

'Pull your collar out, walk on the left,
Those aren't the right shoes, that skirt is too short'
A robot with no emotions.

Thank you for preparing me for the real world,
I'm glad that I got my good grades
And that I made everyone proud
But
That's not the way it should be, is it?

Because everyone has to be the same,
Same grades, same life, same future.
We're all the same.

The girl stands in the doorway,
Streets lined with machines and copies.
She'll be one of those copies soon,
As soon as she steps into that school

Goodbye to my grades,
Goodbye to my life,
Goodbye to my future,
We're all the same.

Alice Dyson (14)
Ysgol Aberconwy, Conwy

Education

Education?
Be robots!
We don't care what you know
As long as your shoes aren't scuffed
Scuffed, scruffed
Do this! Do that!
Be yourself
But not like that!
Look at him!
Look at her!
Bullying will not be tolerated!
But we don't actually care
Unless a parent shouts
Then we promise to sort it out!
Please don't fall!
We can't afford
We can't afford to give you anything
Unless you want a paper towel?
Just wet it,
Don't sweat it!
We want to help
We'll oil you with how to think
To keep your mouth from making a squeak!

Look at you
You're perfect now!
Your metal is shining,
And finally,
Your brain is dead.

Emma Buckley (15)
Ysgol Aberconwy, Conwy

The Predator

A predator in its rightful mind
A child's joyful image at heart,
But when it keeps a child awake at night,
Is it so?

When you're scared to go out in the dark,
Fearful of their fun and games,
It's like living in a circus,
But the joke's on you.

They seem to be everywhere,
Haunting our dreams,
Playing with our mind,
Scaring your soul.

They used to bring happiness,
With their big shoes and their big red nose,
Now it's an elaborate metaphor,
Of what they have become.

They are coming for children,
They are coming for adults,
They are hiding in the dark,
The clowns are coming for you.

Sam Roberts (14)

Ysgol Aberconwy, Conwy

Future

The future, cars that can drive on their own,
No more taxi drivers, not one to phone.

The future, scanners that help you shop
So no more tills, cashiers have
Started to drop.

The future, new machines that can now cook,
Bye bye chefs, a sense of replacement
Is what they took.

The future, roads that don't need to be cared for,
No need for a traffic warden,
Not one to see out of your car door.

The future, robots roaming nearly every street,
Where are the tourists,
The absence of walking feet?

The future, ask yourself, is the transformation worth it?
In this game of new tech,
Eventually you'll have to forfeit.

Cian Whitlow (15)
Ysgol Aberconwy, Conwy

Cake

'Star of the show!'
'Look It's beautiful!'
'Mum, I want that one.'
We all point in awe at the delicately decorated delights.
Made up with powders of sprinkles
And layers of intricate icing.
Perfect.
Perfection.
But to me, they all look the same

The one in the window,
Never left alone
Snap, snap, snap
Every angle, every second
Click, click, click
Picture perfect.
Nobody ever stops talking about it.
'Amazing, awesome, flawless,'
But what does it think about?

Itself?
Who knows?
Who cares?
It's just another cake after all.

April Ehlke-West (14)
Ysgol Aberconwy, Conwy

Autumn

Autumn is one of my favourite seasons
kids are jumping in piles of leaves,
colourful leaves make me smile
because they are one of the best features of autumn.
The naked trees swish in the wind
more leaves falling off trees and more kids
making piles of leaves.

The animals are hibernating in their home,
eating food and sleeping and getting ready
for spring and summer.
When they come out they will collect their food again
I like seeing squirrels collecting their food.

More kids are gathering leaves to make a pile of leaves
and jumping in the piles of leaves.
When they jump in the leaves,
they get more leaves and jump in the leaves.

Jake Ethan Bing (12)
Ysgol Aberconwy, Conwy

Sweet Dreams

My special place... Where I get away from the stress
Of school, of parents, of anything.
My time to connect with others and go back to
The future.

Where my brain comes alive.
He talks to me and I talk back.
Where the silence collides with the noise.
I go where I want.

And no one can stop me or tell me different
Except myself. In a whole new world.
Oblivious to reality. Where to go first?
Skiing in the Sahara or surfing at the snowy summit of
Snowdon?

These are a mere fraction of the supreme
Suggestions to visit. A lifetime of memories.
All I could ever want when really all I'm doing
Is sleeping in my bed.

Benn Lundstram (14)

Ysgol Aberconwy, Conwy

The Monster Under My Bed

When I was younger, everybody warned
me about the monster under my bed.

About his wandering eyes,
and his smirks - what a flirt!

About his loud whistles
that cut into me like thistles.

'It's a compliment!' he yells,
but I hear alarm bells.

He follows me down the road -
I am terrified, and he knows.

Walk faster! Walk faster!
I scream to myself.

My head fills with dread,
he's not under my bed!

Everybody warned me about the monster
under my sheets,

But nobody warned me about the monster
on the streets.

Mary Jones (14)
Ysgol Aberconwy, Conwy

If I Should Die

If I should die,
And you should carry on
And time should grind on
The morning should shine
And moon should burn
As it's always done.

If birds should build as normal,
And bees go buzzing on,
It's hard to think these things will stand
When we, with flowers,
Go on.

That normality will continue
And things go briskly by
Does not make the parting tranquil
Nor ease a clouded goodbye.

That normality will continue
Just keeps a soul in place
To watch the flames rise higher
And make no more
Your trimmings
Of lace.

Charlotte Lewis (15)
Ysgol Aberconwy, Conwy

The Pace Of Life

We grow,
We change,
To be honest it's all a bit strange,
We go from child to adult,
As fast as a lightning bolt.

Does anyone know it's all a big show,
Time goes by,
It's never really that slow.

We grow,
We change,
it's like a book,
And you're turning the page.

You lose friends,
But gain,
It's like a roller coaster that never ends.

You walk by,
You strike a smile,
But as you leave,
I let out a sigh,
I know it's all just one big lie.

A child,
A teen,
An adult,
It all goes by like 1... 2... 3.

Sioned Jones (14)

Ysgol Aberconwy, Conwy

Wars

Wars are horrible, please stop
Nobody likes wars.
Just stop!
Millions of people die,
By guns, tanks, planes, helicopters, people die!

People lose their lives for their countries,
Just stop and help them, they are poor, they don't deserve it,
protect them.
Why do people war for revenge?
No they do it for themselves 'cause they have nothing else
to do.
Why aren't the countries peaceful and happy, just stop
please!

Stop killing, help the world, stop!
Why do you bomb countries?
Stop!
Why do you do it, the countries that are attacked
They can't defend themselves.
Stop wars!

Daniel Godawa (12)

Ysgol Aberconwy, Conwy

Anxiety

My anxiousness held me down to the ground,
The pain of loneliness could not help,
So far down I felt I could not be found,
I wanted to shout, not whimper or yelp.

Enemy OCD made it longer,
Feeling that I am trapped, the only one.
Just needed someone to make me stronger,
My head felt as heavy as one hundred tonne.

But then comes Change, making it look brighter,
I see how I am never by myself.
The weight has been lifted, I float lighter,
I know I'm not the last book on the shelf.

I look up to the sky, I'm back again,
I have found the old me, I've found a friend.

Erin Hughes (12)
Ysgol Aberconwy, Conwy

Worries

The things I worry about,
Are the things that make me cry.
The things I'm scared about,
Will haunt me for life.
Like if my family are OK
Or going to a new place
And getting lost all day.

Things I'm scared about,
Are the things,
That give me butterflies.
The doctor's, dentist and the hospital give me butterflies.

The things I worry about,
Are the things that make me feel small,
When the ones who feel tall,
Come, rain on your parade.

These are the things I worry about,
Are the things that make me cry.
The things I worry about will haunt me for life.

Matilda Cockrill (11)
Ysgol Aberconwy, Conwy

Can I Ever Be A Hero?

I wake up and think
I want to be a hero,
I wouldn't care what colour my suit is, yellow or pink
I just want to be an hero.

I would save everyone
Even in a burning fire
Or in a freezing fridge
And all those criminals would be locked up.

I want to be like Superman
Or maybe Batman might just suit me,
And my weapon could be a pan
Anything would do as long as I could be a hero.

It wouldn't affect my social,
Or school, can't forget that,
I would be a hero in my own time
Or just an hour a day, as long as I could be a hero.

Thomas Taylor (11)
Ysgol Aberconwy, Conwy

Closer

Love can break your heart.
Love can take your soul
Don't give up now it will only grow stronger.
Don't be afraid to love
Don't be afraid of love
Bring your love closer.
But every time I do you break it again.
See the fire in my eyes, it's burning brighter.
Let go of the fear and fly higher and higher
'Cause love can come and go,
And you find the one, hold on tight
But when you let go it is gone.
So pull me closer, as close as you can.
And never let me go.
Closer and closer I go.
And then you back away
And break my heart again.

Stephanie Leigh Stocks (11)
Ysgol Aberconwy, Conwy

Hacker

They will hack you and hunt you down
They will be there when you turn around.
Their mask is scary, it will give you a fright
They will find you and kill you tonight.

There are more of them, about eight
Don't waste your time, it might be too late,
They will butt in the cheating crowd
But sorry they just know.

They talk like robots, don't be fooled
It is not funny and not really cool,
You can't see them down the street
They hide in the shadows of your nightmares
You can barely see them.

Callum Roberts (11)

Ysgol Aberconwy, Conwy

Trick Or Treat

It's as dark as a shadow,
Yet as busy as a bee,
Which door shall we knock on?
I guess we will have to see!

I knocked on the most terrifying, horrifying door of all!
It's number thirteen.
A dark shadow starts to form,
And a packet of sweets,
It's a shame the guy was never seen!

After my bucket is absolutely stuffed,
After an everlasting night,
I seem to have found out,
That number thirteen can actually be alright!

Sophie Maloney (11)
Ysgol Aberconwy, Conwy

Homework

So much homework,
When will it end?
Just look at the pile,
To the side of my bed.

So much to do,
No TV till it's done,
I can't even go out,
To play and run.

Why bother doing it?
It's no use to me,
All it brings,
Is pain and misery.

It's due in tomorrow,
Must get it in on time,
So when Mum tells me to do it,
I just say, 'Fine.'

Rachel Lauren Roberts (14)

Ysgol Aberconwy, Conwy

I Am Scared, But Why?

I am scared that my family will die
I will take back the lies and make them understand,
A flash of light it could arrive.

I am scared of being on my own,
I am scared of big, brutal spiders,
'Nothing more' except the person who lives next door.

Why should we be scared? 'Life is too short!'
You have the whole world to explore.

Macy Hughes (11)
Ysgol Aberconwy, Conwy

Bullying

Bullying is bad
Very, very bad
Don't be a bully
Otherwise you're a crookie
If you're a bully
Go and get a hoody
Because no one likes you
Because you're mean and nasty.
Yeah, go away bully otherwise you're a cookie
Go and get some milk to dip with your Celt
Go big bully, bye bye bully,
Don't come back, only if you got some cookie.

Hannah J (11)
Ysgol Aberconwy, Conwy

Test On Me?

Drugged
Hurt
Mutilated against
Used
Killed
Left in suspense.

Experimentations that don't go right
Heartless humans giving a one-sided fight
Helpless creatures left to die
And the scientist, who won't even cry.

This needs to stop
This is a cry for help
For the animals who are left
To cry, whimper, yelp.

Lana Jessica Davidson-Flood (15)
Ysgol Aberconwy, Conwy

YOUNG WRITERS INFORMATION

We hope you have enjoyed reading this book – and that you will continue to in the coming years.

If you're a young adult who enjoys reading and creative writing, or the parent of an enthusiastic poet or story writer, do visit our website **www.youngwriters.co.uk.** Here you will find free competitions, workshops and games, as well as recommended reads, a poetry glossary and our blog.

If you would like to order further copies of this book, or any of our other titles, then please give us a call or visit **www.youngwriters.co.uk.**

Young Writers
Remus House
Coltsfoot Drive
Peterborough
PE2 9BF
(01733) 890066
info@youngwriters.co.uk